CUTTING THE PAIN AWAY

Understanding Self-Mutilation

- **Anorexia Nervosa:**
  Starving for Attention

- **Child Abuse and Neglect:**
  Examining the Psychological Components

- **Conduct Unbecoming:**
  Hyperactivity, Attention Deficit, and Disruptive Behavior Disorders

- **Cutting the Pain Away:**
  Understanding Self-Mutilation

- **Drowning Our Sorrows:**
  Psychological Effects of Alcohol Abuse

- **Life Out of Focus:**
  Alzheimer's Disease and Related Disorders

- **The Mental Effects of Heroin**

- **Psychological Disorders Related to Designer Drugs**

- **Psychological Effects of Cocaine and Crack Addiction**

- **Schizophrenia:**
  Losing Touch with Reality

- **Sibling Rivalry:**
  Relational Disorders Involving Brothers and Sisters

- **Smoke Screen:**
  Psychological Disorders Related to Nicotine Use

- **Through a Glass Darkly:**
  The Psychological Effects of Marijuana and Hashish

- **The Tortured Mind:**
  The Many Faces of Manic Depression

- **When Families Fail:**
  Psychological Disorders Caused by Parent-Child Relational Problems

- **A World Upside Down and Backwards:**
  Reading and Learning Disorders

THE ENCYCLOPEDIA OF PSYCHOLOGICAL DISORDERS

Senior Consulting Editor Carol C. Nadelson, M.D.
Consulting Editor Claire E. Reinburg

CUTTING THE PAIN AWAY

Understanding Self-Mutilation

Ann Holmes

CHELSEA HOUSE PUBLISHERS
Philadelphia

The ENCYCLOPEDIA OF PSYCHOLOGICAL DISORDERS provides up-to-date information on the history of, causes and effects of, and treatment and therapies for problems affecting the human mind. The titles in this series are not intended to take the place of the professional advice of a psychiatrist or mental health care professional.

Chelsea House Publishers
Editor in Chief: Stephen Reginald
Managing Editor: James D. Gallagher
Production Manager: Pamela Loos
Art Director: Sara Davis
Director of Photography: Judy L. Hasday
Senior Production Editor: LeeAnne Gelletly

Staff for CUTTING THE PAIN AWAY: UNDERSTANDING SELF-MUTILATION
Editorial Assistant: Anne Hill, Bruce Wiener
Picture Researcher: Sandy Jones
Associate Art Director: Takeshi Takahashi
Designer: 21st Century Publishing and Communications, Inc.
Cover Designer: Brian Wible

The ChelseaHouse World Wide Web site address is
http://www.chelseahouse.com

First Printing
1 2 3 4 5 6 7 8 9 10

Library of Congress Cataloging-in-Publication Data

Holmes, Ann.
Cutting the pain away: understanding self-mutilation / Ann Holmes.
92 p. cm. — (Encyclopedia of psychological disorders)
Includes bibliographical references and index.
Summary: Examines the nature, causes, and treatment of self-mutilation and related disorders, as well as ways of helping someone who inflicts self-injuries.
ISBN 0-7910-4951-5 (hc)
1. Self-mutilation Juvenile literature. 2. Teenage girls—Mental health Juvenile literature. 3. Self-injurious behavior Juvenile literature.
[1. Self-mutilation.] I. Title. II. Series.
RJ506.S44H64   1999
616.85'82—dc21   99-19764
                                                                  CIP
                                                                  AC

CONTENTS

PSYCHOLOGICAL DISORDERS AND THEIR EFFECT

CAROL C. NADELSON, M.D.
PRESIDENT AND CHIEF EXECUTIVE OFFICER,
The American Psychiatric Press

There are a wide range of problems that are considered psychological disorders, including mental and emotional disorders, problems related to alcohol and drug abuse, and some diseases that cause both emotional and physical symptoms. Psychological disorders often begin in early childhood, but during adolescence we see a sharp increase in the number of people affected by these disorders. It has been estimated that about 20 percent of the U.S. population will have some form of mental disorder sometime during their lifetime. Some psychological disorders appear following severe stress or trauma. Others appear to occur more often in some families and may have a genetic or inherited component. Still other disorders do not seem to be connected to any cause we can yet identify. There has been a great deal of attention paid to learning about the causes and treatments of these disorders, and exciting new research has taught us a great deal in the past few decades.

The fact that many new and successful treatments are available makes it especially important that we reject old prejudices and outmoded ideas that consider mental disorders to be untreatable. If psychological problems are identified early, it is possible to prevent serious consequences. We should not keep these problems hidden or feel shame that we or a member of our family has a mental disorder. Some people believe that something they said or did caused a mental disorder. Some people think that these disorders are "only in your head" so that you could "snap out of it" if you made the effort. This type of thinking implies that a treatment is a matter of willpower or motivation. It is a terrible burden for someone who is suffering to be blamed for his or her misery, and often people with psychological disorders are not treated compassionately. We hope that the information in this book will teach you about various mental illnesses.

The problems covered in the volumes of the ENCYCLOPEDIA OF PSYCHOLOGICAL DISORDERS were selected because they are of particular importance to young adults, because they affect them directly, or because they affect family and friends. There are individual volumes on reading disorders, attention deficit and disruptive behavior disorders, and dementia—all of these are related to our abilities to learn and integrate information from the world around us. There are books on drug abuse that provide useful information about the effects of these drugs and treatments that are available for those individuals who have drug problems. Some of the books concentrate on one of the most common mental disorders, depression. Others deal with eating disorders, which are dangerous illnesses that affect a large number of young adults, especially women.

Most of the public attention paid to these disorders arises from a particular incident involving a celebrity that awakens us to our own vulnerability to psychological problems. These incidents of celebrities or public figures revealing their own psychological problems can also enable us to think about what we can do to prevent and treat these types of problems.

Self-mutilation—the deliberate harming of skin tissue without suicidal intent—has been called the "addiction of the '90s."

SELF-MUTILATION: AN OVERVIEW

Self-mutilation occurs when a person intentionally damages parts of his or her body. People who harm themselves are typically not trying to commit suicide; instead, their self-mutilation is a method of releasing deeply rooted frustrations. More than two-thirds of the people who mistreat their bodies were at one time victims of sexual or physical abuse. The physical scars left by cutting or burning their flesh indicate the emotional scars that they may hide inside.

Self-mutilation is a growing problem. Studies indicate that 2 million people harm themselves each year. Statistics also show that females are most likely to self-mutilate. They often begin by cutting themselves in their teens.

There are several methods of helping a self-abuser. The most important factor in treatment is the person's willingness to stop hurting himself or herself. Although recovery from self-mutilation may take considerable time and effort, a person who has the strength to survive the trauma that brought on the self-abusive behavior is also mentally equipped to stop injuring his or her body.

This volume of the ENCYCLOPEDIA OF PSYCHOLOGICAL DISORDERS explains the psychological causes of self-mutilation, and its effects on the cutter and his or her family and friends. The book details the treatment and therapy that a cutter must go through in order to stop his or her self-harming behavior, provides ways that a person can delay the need to self-mutilate, and offers advice to loved ones on how to deal with a loved one's self-harm.

Feelings of depression, or anxiety about a traumatic event such as rape or sexual abuse, may lead young women to harm themselves. These harmful actions may include burning or cutting flesh with a razor. Studies show that women are more likely to self-mutilate than men.

1

WHAT IS SELF-INJURY?

When she was 15 years old, Carrie and her best friend were cleaning the pool at her friend's house in their bathing suits. Her friend's older brother came home, then went into the house. "I'd always had kind of a crush on him," Carrie says. "He was cute and older—one of those guys you think you'll never get together with." When Carrie went inside to change for driver's ed class, the brother walked in on her in the bathroom, and they started kissing. Then things went too far. Although she asked him to stop, Carrie says, "He raped me."

Carrie remembers being numb afterward—"To this day, the only thing I remember clearly is taking a shower when I got home," she admitted to Andrea Todd of *Seventeen* magazine—and she didn't sleep for the next two days. On the third day, sitting by herself in the basement, she cried and got drunk. Depressed and upset, she started thinking about suicide. "While I was up in the bathroom, I saw the razor blade," Carrie said. "I took it down with me to the basement and started cutting my wrists."

Carrie knew that the cuts she was making weren't deep enough to kill herself. "It's more like I was trying to sort something out in my head, bringing the razor across my flesh, back and forth," she explained. "The angrier I got, the more I thought about what had happened, the harder I cut."

After that day, whenever Carrie was sad or depressed she would feel the urge to cut herself. She would wait for a time when she was alone, or wouldn't be missed, and then go back to the basement with a razor. She would slash at her arms or legs, then bandage herself. She continued cutting herself for two years, until she was a senior in high school. Finally she confronted her friend about her brother's actions. "She actually said to me, 'Yeah, I heard you screaming but I didn't go in the house,'" Carrie said. "That pushed me right over the edge. I always suspected she knew, and now I knew for sure that she did—but didn't do anything or even ever ask me about it."

Confused and hurt, Carrie talked to her high school counselor, who recommended a local therapist. She met with the psychiatrist and eventually felt comfortable enough to discuss the rape. Her counselor suggested that she attend a group discussion that included others Carrie's age. It was a revelation.

"One of the first things I heard that night was one of the other girls talking about how she cut herself," Carrie recalled. "I had no idea other people did this. I felt so awful for the girl and what she was going through, but I felt so good for myself. I felt less like a freak."

Although Carrie knew that she was damaging her body, she couldn't stop cutting herself. Eventually, her parents and psychiatrist admitted her to a two-month treatment program for people who cut themselves, called "self-injurers."

Self-injury is the deliberate damaging of body tissue—hurting your body on purpose. The injury is often severe enough for tissue damage such as scarring to result. However, it is important to remember that people who self-injure usually do not have a conscious intent to commit suicide; in other words, people who cut themselves like Carrie are generally not attempting to actually kill themselves. Rather, the cutting, burning, or other form of injury is an act intended to relieve tension or cope with depression.

TYPES OF SELF-INJURY

Self-injury—also known as self-mutilation, self-harm, autoaggression, intentional injury, symbolic wounding, masochism, local self-destruction, aggression against the self, parasuicide or focal suicide, deliberate self-harm, delicate self-cutting, and cutting—was classified into three major types in an article published in the February 1993 issue of *Hospital and Community Psychiatry*. These types include major self-mutilation, stereotypic self-mutilation, and superficial (or moderate) self-mutilation.

Major self-mutilation is the most extreme form of self-injury and also the least common. It is called "major" because although the injurious acts occur infrequently, a great deal of tissue is removed or destroyed. This may include self-castration (the cutting out and removal of the genitals); amputation of a limb or extremity, like a hand or foot; or eye gouging. As a result, major self-mutilation often causes permanent disfigurement. It is most often associated with psychotic states or acute drug intoxication.

Stereotypic self-mutilation— fixed, often rhythmic and repetitive, patterns of self- abuse (for example, a person who bangs his head against a hard surface)—is commonly seen in people who have been institutionalized because they are mentally retarded. Stereotypic is one of three classifications of self-mutilation; the others are major self-mutilation, in which severe damage is caused (self-amputation of a limb, castration, or gouging out an eye), and superficial self-mutilation, in which a person cuts or burns him- or herself to express inner pain or frustration or to relieve stress.

Stereotypic self-mutilation consists of fixed, often rhythmic and repetitive, patterns. The most common form of stereotypic self-mutilation is head banging—when a person either hits his head repeatedly against a hard surface, such as a wall or door, or hits himself in the head with an object. "When things were unbearable, [I] slammed the telephone or other objects against my head hard enough to overwhelm the intolerable emotional pain," explained one person. Other forms of stereotypic self-mutilation are pressing thumb or fingers hard against the eyeballs, and biting the fingers or arms. Stereotypic self-mutilation is most commonly seen in the institutionalized mentally retarded, but it also occurs in autistic, psychotic, or schizophrenic people.

Although *superficial self-mutilation* is a significant indicator of emotional distress, this kind of self-injury is not lethal and results in relatively little tissue damage. It occurs occasionally, rather than regularly, but sometimes superficial self-mutilation can develop an addictive

Someone you know may be a "cutter." Specialists estimate that about 2 million people self-mutilate, usually as a coping mechanism.

quality and become an overwhelming preoccupation for its victim. The most common method of superficial self-mutilation is cutting the skin with razor blades or broken glass. Other examples are carving words or symbols into the skin; burning flesh, usually with matches or cigarettes; continual interfering with healing wounds (for example, picking at scabs so they won't heal); sticking needles into the arms, legs, or thighs; punching or pulling hair from the head and body; rubbing glass into the skin; and scratching the skin deeply and continuously. Superficial self-mutilation is the most common form of this self-injury, and the one that this book will focus on. It can be further broken down into three types: compulsive, episodic, and repetitive.

Compulsive self-harm is seen in hair pulling, skin picking, and skin rubbing that is done to remove perceived faults or blemishes in the skin. These acts may be part of an obsessive-compulsive disorder ritual involving obsessional thoughts—the person tries to relieve tension and prevent some bad thing from happening by engaging in self-harm. (Obsessive-compulsive disorder is a psychological disturbance marked by persistent unwanted thoughts—the obsession—coupled with behavior that becomes repetitive. This behavior—the compulsion—is designed to ease feelings of discomfort or dread.) Compulsive self-harm has a somewhat different nature and different roots from the episodic and repetitive types.

The difference between episodic and repetitive self-harm seems to be a matter of degree. Episodic self-harm is self-injurious behavior engaged in occasionally by people who don't think about it otherwise and don't see themselves as self-injurers. It generally is a symptom of some other psychological disorder. However, what begins as occasional, episodic self-harm can become repetitive self-harm. Repetitive self-harm is marked by a shift toward thinking about self-injury even when not actually doing it, and recognizing oneself as a self-injurer. Episodic self-harm becomes repetitive when what was first a symptom becomes a disease in itself. Many people who self-injure describe self-harm as addictive.

Superficial self-mutilation is a fairly common problem. Dr. Armando Favazza, a professor of psychiatry at the University of Missouri–Columbia School of Medicine and the author of *Bodies Under Siege*, the first comprehensive exploration of self-injury, estimates that in the United States 750 people per 100,000 population, or about 2 million people, exhibit moderate self-injurious behavior. Marilee Strong, who interviewed nearly 100 self-injurers for her 1998 book, *A Bright Red Scream*, calls it "the addiction of the '90s."

The typical person who self-mutilates is a young intelligent woman from a middle- or upper-class background. Many cutters have a background of childhood trauma, such as physical or sexual abuse.

2

WHO SELF-INJURES AND WHY DO THEY DO IT?

Self-injury can take many forms. But what kind of people consider self-injury, then actually take the next step and cut themselves? And why do they do it?

It is estimated that about 2 million people in the United States self-injure. This number encompasses people from all walks of life, from actor Johnny Depp to teenagers in every community, such as "Ella":

> Ella was having a bad summer. She was depressed and angry because her boyfriend was not spending time with her, and she had been seeing a psychiatrist, dealing with the fact she had been sexually abused when she was five years old. "I was having flashbacks. I was home alone, feeling like no one was helping me." The scissors were "just there. . . . I just sliced my arms aimlessly, crying hysterically."
>
> After this, any time that Ella felt angry or lonely, she would cut herself and then bandage the wounds. "It's like I was literally trying to show someone how much I was hurting," she said later. "I was making the internal pain external." When cutting wasn't enough to end her emotional pain, Ella started burning herself, too. "I had a cigarette, and I remember looking at it and thinking, Oh! A new way!" she recalled.
>
> Her depression kept her from graduating from high school, affected her relationship with her boyfriend, and eventually caused her to seek treatment. Doctors at the clinic where she stayed for several months were pleased with her progress in therapy and released her; however, back at home she couldn't stop cutting herself—until she learned that her half brother was in the hospital, recovering from surgery to remove a brain tumor.
>
> "Seeing him with that scar across his head made me stop thinking about my own problems and start thinking about what I was doing to myself,"

she said. "Also, I was staying at the time with my real brother, who was 11 when I was being abused and knew about it and didn't do anything. We talked about it—I confronted him, I guess—and he apologized. It's like something was fixed."

Ella's story is not uncommon. In fact, she apparently is a typical victim of this disorder. From the results of one study of self-mutilation (Favazza and Conterio, 1986) a portrait of the typical self-injurer can be drawn. According to this study, the typical victim is female (97 percent of the study participants were women) and usually begins cutting herself in her teens, generally around age 14, continuing to injure herself, often with increasing severity, into her late twenties and early thirties. In some cases the participants also suffered from eating disorders such as anorexia nervosa or bulimia. The self-injurer tends to be from a middle- or upper-middle-class background, and is often intelligent and well educated. However, more than two-thirds of the women studied came from a background of sexual or physical abuse, or had at least one alcoholic parent.

The most common form of self-injury was cutting (72 percent), followed by burning (35 percent), self-hitting (30 percent), interference with wound healing (22 percent), hair pulling (10 percent), and bone breaking (8 percent). About 78 percent of the women studied used more than one method of self-injury. On average, survey respondents admitted to 50 acts of self-mutilation, and two-thirds admitted to having cut, burned, or otherwise hurt themselves within the past month.

There are several other psychological characteristics that have been noted in self-injurers. These individuals may have strong feelings of self-loathing or may feel that they are "not good enough" when compared to parents or peers. They may be hypersensitive to rejection. Self-injurers may seem to be constantly angry (usually with themselves) or have aggressive feelings; however, they tend to suppress these feelings or direct them inward.

Self-injurers tend to be impulsive, acting as their mood of the moment directs. They also tend not to plan for the future, are depressed and suicidal or self-destructive, suffer chronic anxiety, and tend to be irritable. In addition, they do not sense that they have much control over their life and do not see themselves as skilled at coping, and in fact they usually do not have a variety of coping skills.

Actor Johnny Depp, the star of such movies as Edward Scissorhands *and* Donnie Brasco, *has admitted dealing with feelings through self-harming behavior. Depp has also gained a "bad boy" reputation for taking out negative frustrations by destroying hotel rooms and getting into fights.*

WHY DO PEOPLE HARM THEMSELVES?

Ironically, people cut or injure themselves because it makes them feel better mentally; the physical pain helps blot a psychic pain or anxiety. As one victim, a popular 16-year-old cheerleader, explained: "I had so much anxiety, I couldn't concentrate on anything until I somehow let that out, and not being able to let it out in words, I took the razor and started cutting my leg and I got excited about seeing my blood. It felt good to see the blood coming out, like my other pain was leaving, too." The injury may also help relieve feelings of anger.

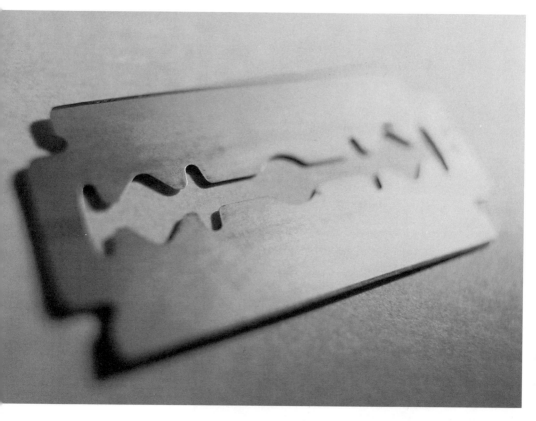

The most common form of self-injury is cutting; 72 percent of people who harm themselves use razor blades, knives, broken glass, or another sharp implement to cut their skin. Other methods include burning, hitting themself with a hard object, picking at scabs, or pulling hair. About 78 percent of self-mutilators use more than one method to self-injure.

Self-injury may also help a person establish a feeling of control in his or her life. In other words, the person feels that cutting is something he or she can decide. (This mentality is seen in eating disorders as well). Self-injury for control may be more common among teens than adults, because teens with overbearing parents may feel they are being denied control in every other area of their life.

Another reason people injure themselves is that it can jolt them out of states of numbness or emptiness, and make them feel alive. As one patient explained, "There have been times when I don't even feel like I'm alive. I'll do something to feel—anything. And that's usually cutting. Just seeing blood."

These states of numbness may be linked to painful memories of abuse, and there may be an explanation for cutting, burning, or other injurious actions as a reaction to a traumatic event. Cutting and other types of self-injury often occur following an event that causes a sense of loss or abandonment; social isolation, confinement, or helplessness; rejection; failure; anger; or guilt. When a person is being abused or hurt, a common coping mechanism is to mentally dissociate him- or herself from the situation. By doing this, the person's mental self is separated from the body that is being hurt. The jolt of pain or the welling of blood that occurs with self-injury somehow helps reestablish the mental and physical connection that was separated during the trauma.

SEXUAL ABUSE AND SELF-MUTILATION

People who injure themselves are likely to have suffered sexual abuse when they were younger. Child sexual abuse is any sexual behavior directed toward a child or adolescent under 18 by a person who has power over that youth. Such behavior always involves a betrayal of the child's trust. The forms of sexual abuse that involve physical contact could include fondling the child's genitals, getting the child to fondle the offender's genitals, rubbing the abuser's genitals on the child, engaging in oral sex, or making anal or vaginal penetration. There are also non-physical forms of sexual abuse, including exhibitionism (when a person shows his or her genitals to a child), the showing of pornography (sexually explicit pictures or videotapes) to a child, the involvement of a child in creating pornographic materials, and sexual suggestiveness.

In the 1986 Favazza and Conterio study mentioned earlier, 65 percent of the women reported being sexually abused as children. In 1989 an article published in the *American Journal of Psychiatry* provided more support for the theory that physical or sexual abuse or trauma is an important antecedent to self-mutilation. The article reviewed the cases of three women who became self-cutters following a traumatic rape. Before the sexual assault none had tendencies to self-injure (Greenspan and Samuel, 1989).

Another study that year (Herman, Perry, and Van der Kolk, 1989) examined patients who had exhibited cutting behavior or suicidal tendencies. The study concluded that the amount and the severity of cutting could be predicted based on the levels of physical or sexual abuse, physical or emotional neglect, and chaotic family conditions during childhood and adolescence. Victims of sexual abuse were found most likely to self-injure.

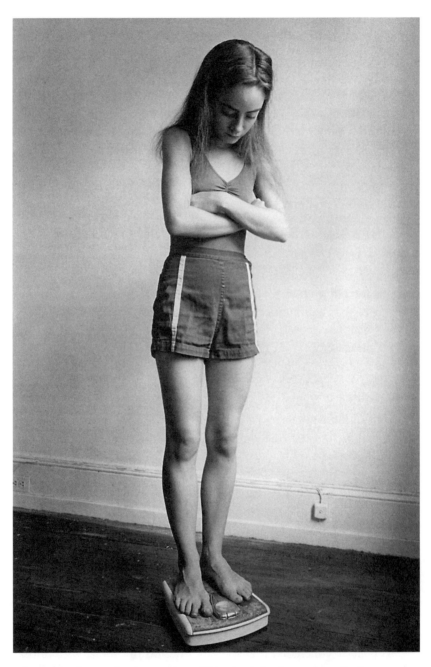

It is common for people who practice self-harming behavior to also suffer from an eating disorder such as anorexia nervosa, bulimia, or compulsive overeating. Some studies indicate that eating disorders and self-mutilation have similar causes.

The earlier the abuse started, the more likely the subjects of the study were to cut themselves; these people also injured themselves more severely.

These findings indicate that sexual abuse in childhood can lead a person to self-mutilate. However, not all victims of sexual abuse release their feelings about the traumatic event through self-injurious acts; just as many of those who hurt themselves have suffered no childhood abuse.

INVALIDATING ENVIRONMENTS

Another important factor that contributes to self-mutilation centers on the patient having grown up in an "invalidating environment"—one in which the person is not seen as having legitimate or valid feelings or opinions. Though an abusive home certainly qualifies as invalidating, so do other normal situations.

In an invalidating environment, when a child tries to communicate feelings or talk about experiences, his or her parents do not validate those feelings. In other words, the parental response does not accept those feelings or experiences as truthful. The adult reacts erratically, inappropriately, or extremely, by punishing, trivializing, and/or dismissing the child's feelings or experiences.

Invalidation sends the child two messages. First, it tells the individual that he or she is wrong in both describing and analyzing the experiences and views that are causing his or her emotions, beliefs, and actions. Second, it attributes his or her experiences to socially unacceptable characteristics or personality traits.

This invalidation can take many forms. Here are some common verbal ones:

"You're angry but you just won't admit it."

"You really did do it. Stop lying."

"You're being hypersensitive."

"You're just lazy."

"I won't let you manipulate me like that."

"Cheer up. Snap out of it. You can get over this."

"If you'd just look on the bright side and stop being a pessimist . . ."

"You're just not trying hard enough."

"I'll give you something to cry about!"

PRINCESS DIANA

Although she was rich, beautiful, and loved by millions of people, Princess Diana was unhappy in her marriage. The princess suffered from the eating disorder bulimia and cut herself on several occasions to alleviate the pain she was feeling.

I t is difficult to imagine a person more loved than the late Diana, Princess of Wales. She was one of the most photographed people in the world, and was admired by millions of people. However, despite the world's admiration, Diana's life was not always perfect, or even happy. When she was a young girl,

Everyone experiences invalidations like these at some time or another, but for people brought up in invalidating environments, these messages are constantly received. Parents may mean well but are too uncomfortable with negative emotion to allow their children to express it, and the result is unintentional invalidation. This in turn can lead to negative

her parents divorced. In 1981, as a beautiful but shy 20-year-old woman, she married Charles, Prince of Wales and heir to the throne of England—certainly the world's most eligible bachelor. But even though Diana immediately became the most popular member of the Royal Family, she found herself increasingly stressed and stifled by the demands of court life and the pressure of constant media attention. Also, although Charles and Diana had two sons, their marriage was not happy.

After she became pregnant with her first child, William, Diana's feeling of being trapped began to manifest itself as self-harm. She slashed at her wrists with a razor blade, threw herself against a glass display case at Kensington Palace, and cut herself with a lemon slicer, according to biographer Andrew Morton. "On yet another occasion, during a heated argument with Prince Charles, she picked up a penknife lying on his dressing table and cut her chest and her thighs," Morton wrote in his 1992 book, *Diana: Her True Story*. Morton's biography also chronicled Diana's longtime struggle with the eating disorder bulimia nervosa and her five suicide attempts. These cries for help were ignored by her husband and the rest of the Royal Family, who felt that they were attention-getting ploys.

In 1992 Diana and Charles separated, and she underwent therapy for her eating disorder and self-mutilation. In 1996 she divorced the prince and began a new life. She increased the charity work that she had begun years earlier, working especially with AIDS victims and toward an international ban on the use of land mines. When she died in a automobile crash in September 1997, two million people attended a funeral procession for the People's Princess and two billion more watched the day's sad events on television.

feelings of "I never mattered," or feelings that "I don't have any 'real' problems." This feeling that the person doesn't deserve to feel sorry for himself or herself, or doesn't deserve attention, can lead to a vicious cycle: self-hate and a need to punish himself or herself for having the invalidated emotions in the first place.

Physical or sexual abuse are common among women who self-mutilate: one study indicated that 65 percent of cutters were sexually abused as children. Another study concluded that the amount and severity of self-harming behavior could be predicted, based on the level of childhood abuse or neglect.

BIOLOGICAL CAUSES OF SELF-INJURY

Some research has indicated that there may be a biological component to self-injurious behavior. Studies show that variations in certain chemicals created naturally in the brain may cause increased feelings of aggression and may lead people to harm themselves.

Neurotransmitters are chemicals that pass messages to and from nerve cells. They are a key component in the way that information from the body (pain, pleasure, warmth, etc.) is passed to the brain and throughout the central nervous system. The spaces between nerve cells are called *synapses*; neurotransmitters carry the nerve's message, in the form of an electrical impulse, across these spaces.

Different neurotransmitter receptors affect different bodily functions. Scientists have found that the functions of a neurotransmitter called *serotonin* include regulating emotion, mood, impulsivity, aggression, digestion, smooth muscle relaxation, and sexual behavior. Decreases in the body's serotonin level have been linked to increased irritation and aggression.

In 1991 scientists found that drugs that help the brain to create serotonin, thus increasing its level in a person's body, also help to reduce self-harming behavior. The report concluded that there is a relationship between self-injury and obsessive-compulsive disorder, which in fact is often treated with serotonin-enhancing drugs (Winchel and Stanley, 1991). In another study two years later, researchers linked low serotonin levels to depression. Since depression is one of the consequences of childhood physical abuse, the study concluded that low serotonin may be one reason self-mutilation is seen more frequently among those abused as children than among the general population (Malinosky-Rummel and Hanson, 1993).

Most recently, a 1997 study concluded that serotonin's main behavioral effect is on irritability, and that the type of aggressive behavior shown in response to irritation seems to be dependent on levels of serotonin. For example, if a person's serotonin level is normal, irritability may be expressed by yelling or throwing things, but if the level of serotonin is low, responses to irritation escalate into attacks on others, self-injury, or, in some cases, suicide.

Obviously a person's serotonin level is just one factor that can affect whether or not he or she practices self-injurious behavior. Also, scientists are undecided about the cause of reduced serotonin: Does it occur as a result of abuse or invalidation? Or do people who cut or harm themselves have naturally low serotonin levels?

A person's low self-esteem, often linked to his or her childhood history, can lead to self-mutilation. Currently, self-harm is not considered a separate psychological disorder but a component of other disorders.

3

SELF-MUTILATION AND RELATED DISORDERS

A t the present time, self-mutilation is not classified as a psychological disorder by the American Psychiatric Association (APA). Rather, the APA's comprehensive reference work on psychological problems, the *Diagnostic and Statistical Manual of Mental Disorders*, Fourth Edition (often referred to as the *DSM-IV*), includes self-mutilative acts as part of another psychological problem called borderline personality disorder.

BORDERLINE PERSONALITY DISORDER

This disorder is characterized by a pattern of unstable relationships, impulsive behavior, and sudden or dramatic shifts in self-image. According to the *DSM-IV*, a patient must meet five of nine criteria for a doctor to diagnose borderline personality disorder. These criteria include:

1. Frantic efforts to avoid real or imagined abandonment

2. A pattern of unstable and intense interpersonal relationships characterized by alternating between extremes of idealization and devaluation

3. Identity disturbance (markedly and persistently unstable self-image)

4. Impulsivity in at least two areas that are potentially self-damaging (for example, spending, sex, substance abuse, reckless driving, or binge eating)

5. Recurrent suicidal behavior or threats of suicide, or self-mutilating behavior

6. Instability due to mood changes (such as intense sadness or depression, anxiety, or irritability)

7. Chronic feelings of emptiness

8. Inappropriate, intense anger or difficulty controlling feelings of anger (this can be indicated by frequent displays of temper or recurrent physical fights)

9. Brief occurrences of paranoid feelings or dissociative disorder

Regarding criteria 4 and 5, the *DSM-IV* reports:

> Individuals with Borderline Personality Disorder display impulsivity in at least two areas that are potentially self-damaging. They may gamble, spend money irresponsibly, binge eat, abuse substances,
>
> engage in unsafe sex, or drive recklessly. Individuals with Borderline Personality Disorder display recurrent suicidal behavior, gestures, or threats, or self-mutilating behavior. Completed suicide occurs in 8%–10% of such individuals, and self-mutilative acts (e.g., cutting or burning) and suicide threats and attempts are very common. Recurrent suicidality is often the reason that these students [seek] help. . . . Self-mutilation may occur during dissociative experiences and often brings relief by reaffirming the ability to feel or by expiating the individual's sense of being evil.

Many of the traits and statistics common to self-mutilation can be seen in people with borderline personality disorder. For example, the *DSM-IV* says that about 75 percent of people diagnosed with this problem are females. (As Chapter 2 noted, a large percentage of people who self-harm are young women.) The *DSM-IV* also reports, "Physical and sexual abuse, neglect, hostile conflict, and early parental loss or separation are more common in the childhood histories of those with Borderline Personality Disorder." These experiences are all common in the histories of people who self-mutilate as well. And the *DSM-IV* says that "the impairment from the disorder [is] greatest in the young adult years and gradually wane[s] with advancing age. During their thirties and forties, the majority of individuals with this disorder attain greater stability in their relationships and [jobs]." Again, this is similar to the conclusions reached in Favazza and Conterio's 1986 study, which indicated that women typically ended their self-harming behavior as they grew older.

However, there is some evidence that borderline personality disorder is often misdiagnosed. A 1992 study of 89 patients diagnosed with borderline personality disorder found that only 36 had met the *DSM-IV* criteria (five of nine symptoms from the above list) required for diagnosis. This indicates that borderline personality disorder may be overdiagnosed—that perhaps some doctors misclassify their "problem" patients as borderline personality.

OBSESSIVE-COMPULSIVE DISORDER

Some psychiatrists feel that a psychological disorder called obsessive-compulsive disorder may also cause, or lead to, self-harming behavior. Obsessive-compulsive disorder is characterized by recurrent obsessions or compulsions that are severe and cause the person distress or impairment. Obsessions are persistent ideas, thoughts, impulses, or images that are not necessarily related to a real-life problem, but that bother the person, who believes they are intrusive and inappropriate. Some examples of common obsessions include: repeated thoughts about cleanliness or fears about contamination (by shaking hands or touching a doorknob, for example); repeated doubts about whether or not the person has performed some action, such as leaving a door unlocked or a stove on; a need to have things in a particular order, and feelings of distress when objects are not in that order; and aggressive impulses, such as a desire to hurt someone or to shout something obscene in church, for example. A person with obsessions attempts to ignore or suppress his or her thoughts, or to neutralize them with another action or thought. This is a compulsion. The person who fears continuously that he or she left the stove on might neutralize these fears by checking the stove continuously to make sure that it is turned off.

Compulsions could include behaviors (checking the stove or constantly washing one's hands) or mental acts (praying, counting, or repeating words silently) that are intended to reduce anxiety or stress. The *DSM-IV* notes:

> In most cases, the person feels driven to perform the compulsion to reduce the distress that accompanies an obsession or to prevent some dreaded event or situation. For example, individuals with obsessions about being contaminated may reduce their mental distress by washing their hands until their skin is raw; individuals distressed by obsessions about having left a door unlocked may be driven to check the lock every few minutes; individuals distressed by unwanted blasphemous thoughts may find relief in counting to 10 backward and forward 100 times for each thought. In some cases, individuals perform rigid or stereotyped acts according to idiosyncratically elaborated rules without being able to indicate why they are doing them. By definition, compulsions are either clearly excessive or are not connected in a realistic way with what they are designed to neutralize or prevent."

Impulsive and risky sexual behavior, and recurrent fights or problems with family or other interpersonal relationships are among the nine criteria for diagnosing borderline personality disorder. Self-mutilation is another of the criteria; a patient must exhibit five of the nine behaviors to be diagnosed as having borderline personality disorder.

Compulsive wringing of hands or constant washing because of fears about being unclean may be a sign of obsessive-compulsive disorder. The obsessions or compulsions are often driven by some past trauma.

Among people who have been diagnosed with obsessive-compulsive disorder, self-injury usually takes the form of trichotillomania (compulsive pulling at head and body hair) or compulsive picking or scratching at skin. Obsessive-compulsive disorder is believed to be caused by a serotonin imbalance in the brain; as discussed in Chapter 2, reduced serotonin can also lead to self-injurious behavior.

SELF-INJURY AS A SEPARATE DISORDER

In February 1993 Dr. Armando Favazza and Dr. Richard Rosenthal published the results of a lengthy study of self-mutilation in *Hospital and Community Psychiatry.* They examined self-harm both as a symptom of other mental disorders, such as borderline personality disorder, and as a distinct syndrome. In addition to their own studies of self-mutilation, Favazza and Rosenthal reviewed data from more than 250 articles and books and incorporated this material into their research.

Favazza and Rosenthal divided self-mutilation into the three basic types that were explained in the first chapter of this book—major, stereotypic, and superficial (or moderate)—and proposed that a syndrome of repetitive superficial self-mutilation should be regarded as a separate psychological disorder, classified under the *DSM-IV* subsection of "Impulse Disorders." They described the disorder as follows:

> The disorder usually begins in late childhood and early adolescence. It waxes and wanes and may become chronic. In many patients the disorder ends after 10 to 15 years, although isolated episodes of self-mutilative behavior may persist. When an eating disorder or alcohol abuse develops, self-mutilative behavior often diminishes but may return as the eating disorder or alcohol abuse abates. In some persons these impulsive behaviors occur simultaneously. . . . The proposed diagnosis of repetitive self-mutilation contains all the essential features of an impulse disorder. The criteria include a failure to resist an impulse, drive, or temptation to perform a harmful act; an increasing sense of tension or arousal prior to the act; and an experience of either pleasure, gratification, or release at the time of the act. Immediately after the act, there may or may not be genuine regret, self-reproach, or guilt.

Their article outlined criteria for the disorder to be diagnosed, as the *DSM-IV* does. The Favazza and Rosenthal criteria are:

1. Preoccupation with harming oneself physically
2. Recurrent failure to resist impulses to harm oneself physically, resulting in the destruction or alteration of body tissue
3. Increasing sense of tension immediately before the act of self-harm
4. Gratification or a sense of relief when committing the act of self-harm
5. The act of self-harm is not associated with conscious suicidal intent and is not in response to a delusion, hallucination, or transsexual fixed idea, or serious mental retardation

According to their article, however, nonrepetitive self-mutilation that occurs with borderline personality disorder or obsessive-compulsive disorder would continue to be considered a symptom of those disorders, rather than as a separate syndrome.

PSYCHOLOGICAL DISORDERS RELATED TO SELF-MUTILATION

When a person self-mutilates, there is a good chance that he or she is afflicted with one or more additional psychological disorders. These may include post-traumatic stress disorder, dissociative identity disorder, and eating disorders. A common variable in each of these related psychological disorders is that they are caused by periods of trauma or intense stress. Each of these disorders can be treated and should be addressed by the doctor or therapist along with the person's self-mutilative behavior.

POST-TRAUMATIC STRESS DISORDER

Among the problems commonly associated with self-mutilation are symptoms of post-traumatic stress disorder. This disorder is also common in children who have been physically or sexually abused or neglected. A person who suffers from this condition may experience the following symptoms:

- Intrusive, distressing memories and dreams of a traumatic event (such as sexual abuse)

- A desire to avoid people, places, situations, or activities that would remind the person about the traumatic event

- Diminished interest in previously enjoyed activities, estrangement from other people, or an inability to feel emotions involving intimacy and tenderness (this is called *psychic numbing* or *emotional anesthesia*)

- Persistent feelings of anxiety, irritability, and anger

According to the *DSM-IV*, some traumatic events that could cause post-traumatic stress disorder include military combat, sexual assault, a physical attack such as a mugging or robbery, an episode of being kidnapped or taken hostage, torture, natural or man-made disaster, severe automobile accident, or the diagnosis of a life-threatening condition.

It is common for a young person who has been abused or suffered a traumatic experience to suffer from post-traumatic stress disorder. The symptoms of this disorder are often seen in people who self-mutilate.

The *DSM-IV* states that the traumatic event can be reexperienced in several ways:

> Commonly the person has recurrent and intrusive recollections of the event or recurrent distressing dreams during which the event is replayed. In rare instances, the person experiences dissociative

states that last from a few seconds to several hours, or even days, during which components of the event are relived and the person behaves as though experiencing the event at that moment. Intense psychological distress or [a physical reaction] often occurs when the person is exposed to triggering events that resemble or symbolize an aspect of the traumatic event.

Some people who have been sexually abused may try to handle their emotional pain by withdrawing from others, thereby avoiding the threat of pain that interpersonal relationships hold. Others may turn to self-harming behavior as an outlet for their feelings. Either way, the person suffers emotional and psychological damage. A large-scale study of 12- to 17-year-olds indicates that out of the 5.7 million adolescents in the United States today who have been victims of either serious sexual assault or serious physical assault, nearly 2 million have suffered from post-traumatic stress disorder, and more than 1 million still suffer from it.

DISSOCIATIVE IDENTITY DISORDER

As the *DSM-IV* notes above, post-traumatic stress disorder can cause a person to experience dissociative states. Dissociation is a mental process that disconnects a person's thoughts, memories, feelings, actions, or sense of identity from present experiences. Most people experience mild dissociations, such as daydreaming or "getting lost" in a book or movie, both of which involve losing touch with conscious awareness of one's immediate surroundings. However, those who suffer from extreme chronic dissociation in response to a traumatic event or series of events may become seriously forgetful and endure periods of amnesia, blackouts, and a severe inability to function in daily activities.

The 1973 case of Sybil Isabel Dorsett, which was turned into a book and a major film, introduced the term "multiple personality disorder." As a result of both horrific child abuse by her psychotic mother and her father's failure to rescue her from the abuse, Sybil's personality "split" into multiple personalities. Each of her 16 distinct personalities, 2 of whom were male, embodied feelings and emotions with which the "real" Sybil could not cope. Sybil herself was deprived of all these emotions and was therefore a rather drab figure. She was also unaware of her split personality. In certain situations Sybil's various personalities

Dissociation is a mental process that disconnects a person's thoughts, memories, feelings, actions, or sense of identity from present experiences. Most people experience mild dissociations; however, those who suffer from extreme chronic dissociation in response to a traumatic event or series of events may become seriously forgetful and endure periods of amnesia or blackouts, and have a severe inability to function in daily activities.

would appear. While these personas were in control of her body, Sybil suffered blackouts and did not remember the episodes. It was only after meeting with a psychoanalyst that Sybil became aware of her multiple personalities.

Sybil's condition has since been renamed *dissociative identity disorder* (DID). The American Psychiatric Association changed the name in response to the highly emotional controversy surrounding such a diagnosis. Critics contended that "multiple personality" was misleading, as it implied several separate individuals occupying one person's body. In fact, only one person inhabits each body, and although the alternate personality states may appear to be very different, they are all manifestations of the single person.

People who chronically dissociate often refer to the experience as "spacing out" or "trancing." Such a reaction provides a temporary mental escape from the fear and pain of the trauma, and in some cases a memory gap occurs surrounding the experience. When faced with overwhelmingly traumatic situations from which there is no physical escape, a person may resort to "going away" in his or her head to avoid both the immediate physical and emotional pain and the anxious anticipation of that pain. By this dissociative process, the thoughts, feelings, memories, and perceptions of the traumatic experience can be separated psychologically, allowing the person to function as if the trauma had not occurred. Over time, however, this mental escape can nearly become a personality trait, invoked whenever the person feels threatened or anxious.

Repeated dissociation can result in a series of separate identities, or mental states, like those developed by Sybil. Dissociative disorders also can lead to depression, mood swings, and suicidal tendencies. Some sufferers have experienced insomnia, night terrors, and sleepwalking, as well as alcohol and drug abuse, auditory and visual hallucinations, and eating disorders.

In 1995 Dr. Beth Brodsky, Dr. Marylene Cloitre, and Dr. Rebecca Dulit studied 60 females who had been admitted to a hospital and diagnosed with borderline personality disorder. Of these patients, 50 percent had experienced severe dissociation, and 52 percent reported a history of self-mutilation. "The subjects who dissociated were more likely than those who did not to self-mutilate and to report childhood abuse," the doctors wrote in their study, published in the December

1995 issue of *American Journal of Psychiatry.* "They also had higher levels of current depressive symptoms and psychiatric treatment. . . . Self-mutilation was the most powerful predictor of dissociation." The study concluded that "Female inpatients with borderline personality disorder who dissociate may represent a sizable subgroup of patients with the disorder who are at especially high risk for self-mutilation, childhood abuse, depression, and utilization of psychiatric treatment."

EATING DISORDERS

It is common for people who practice self-harming behavior to also suffer from an eating disorder such as anorexia nervosa, bulimia, or compulsive overeating. One example is Princess Diana, profiled in the previous chapter, who battled bulimia for many years while also self-injuring.

Anorexia nervosa is an eating disorder that is characterized by a fear of gaining weight. People with this disease may feel fat, even though their actual body weight could be as much as 15 percent below the norm for their age and size. Some anorexics, such as singer Karen Carpenter and gymnast Christy Heinrich, have literally starved themselves to death.

People with anorexia may appear extremely scrawny and undernourished. In the worst cases they seem to be little more than skin tightly stretched over bones. Their skin may appear yellowish and rough. Their blood pressure can become erratic, and their continued starvation can alter the physical construction of the brain. They may feel tired all the time (this is caused by blood anemia) but not be able to rest comfortably, because their sleep patterns become disturbed or irregular.

Anorexia is similar to self-mutilation in many respects. Generally, anorexia occurs in women (between 90 and 95 percent of anorexics are female) who are young adults (the disease usually develops during the mid- to late teens). As with self-mutilation, the main causes of anorexia include stress and childhood trauma or sexual abuse. Anorexics attempt to exert a measure of control over their life by controlling what they eat and how much they weigh, just as cutters attempt to control their psychological suffering through use of physical pain.

Bulimia is more common than anorexia, and it appears in women who, on average, are older than anorexics. In fact, it is fairly common for

The eating disorder anorexia nervosa is similar to self-mutilation in some ways. Both primarily affect women who are in their teens or early twenties, and the main causes of each are stress, childhood trauma, or sexual abuse. Anorexics attempt to exert a measure of control over their lives by controlling what they eat and how much they weigh, just as cutters attempt to control their psychological pain through use of physical pain.

a person to have both disorders simultaneously; about 50 percent of anorexics also suffer from bulimia. People with bulimia nervosa engage in regular periods of "bingeing," or eating a large amount of food at once; bulimics then force themselves to vomit the food they have just eaten, a procedure called "purging." This purging, usually done at least once a day, can be uncomfortable or even painful, but for some bulimics it offers relief from their emotional stress—just as cutting or burning does for a person who self-mutilates. Like anorexia, the binge-and-purge cycle is an attempt to control an aspect of the bulimic's life, because other areas may seem to be out of his or her control.

Compulsive overeating is similar to bulimia, except that a person with this disorder does not purge. As with other eating disorders, compulsive overeaters gorge themselves to combat stress.

Both compulsive overeating and bulimia can cause physical damage to a person's body. Because the overeater may become 20 to 30 percent overweight, heart problems can develop, along with high blood pressure and diabetes. Bulimia can cause weakness, muscle cramps, dizziness, damage to the esophagus, and dehydration. Frequent vomiting can cause stomach acid to damage or ruin tooth enamel. More serious side effects include colon or heart failure.

In order to stop self-mutilating, a cutter must make a conscious decision not to harm herself anymore in order to deal with pain.

4

TREATMENT AND THERAPIES

Loralei began cutting herself after a traumatic move to the United States from South Africa. She had an extremely difficult time adjusting to public high school and found it relaxing to pick at pimples and clogged pores. One day she began cutting herself with a sewing kit she found in the bathroom, and soon she made a ritual out of cutting herself. When the bleeding didn't stop after a particularly deep cut, she went to the emergency room and, after being treated, met the hospital psychiatrist. Having entered therapy, she now realizes that she can ask for help when she needs it. "I've learned new, healthier ways of expressing my feelings. Now when the razor calls, I play my violin or cello, compose music, or call one of my new friends. I realize I may be fighting the urge to cut for the rest of my life, but my flesh and blood are worth it."

Like Loralei, Carrie and Ella (the two young women whose cases were described in previous chapters) also arrived at a moment when they realized they had to stop cutting themselves. Ella decided she didn't want a life of "wanting to die" when she witnessed her brother fighting a brain tumor. Carrie was shocked when, at her doctor's office one day, she saw the arms of a woman who had been cutting for years. "There wasn't even any skin color. It was all scar tissue, bright pinkish, horrifying," she said. "It hit me that if I kept cutting myself—and if I didn't kill myself in the process—that's what I would look like." There are a number of treatment and therapeutic options that can help a self-injurer, but the most important key to successful treatment is that the patient, like Loralei, Carrie, and Ella, must make a decision to stop and want to be in the therapy program.

Self-mutilation is a powerful coping mechanism, and in order to help those who self-injure, therapists must understand what role it plays in their clients' lives. Is cutting, burning, or other forms of self-injury primarily a means of releasing tension? Communicating? Dealing with painful experiences? Understanding why a particular person self-injures is the key to helping that person stop using self-harm as a way to cope. Therapists also need to examine their own motives for wanting a client to cease self-injury. Care providers may focus on stopping the self-injury as quickly as possible because they themselves are not comfortable with it—it repulses or frightens them and makes them feel ineffective. This may lead to a power struggle in which the therapist insists that the behavior stop and the client chooses to self-injure secretly, becoming distrustful and reducing the chance that a useful therapeutic partnership will result.

On the other hand, it is legitimate for therapists to help clients devise some sort of plan for dealing with their impulses to cut or harm themselves, and to help stabilize their lives. When a client is engaging in uncontrolled self-injury, the injury takes center stage in therapy, leaving no room for dealing with core issues that are causing the patient to self-injure. Therapists must walk a fine line between attempting to get all self-injurious behavior under control and not allowing the self-injury to become the focus of the therapy.

One approach might be where self-injury is tolerated but has specific consequences. For example, a client might be invited to contact the therapist when an urge to self-harm occurs, but restricted from contact for 24 hours after an actual self-injurious act. In a system like this the self-injurer can communicate without having to resort to self-injury, and she knows that if she gives in to her urge to harm herself, there will be tangible and immediate (but not permanent) negative effects. This kind of agreement between therapist and client can help stabilize the self-injury and clear the road for dealing with the issues underlying the need to injure, allowing the therapist to treat self-harm within the context of the underlying cause.

If necessary, therapists should ensure that self-injuring clients have access to nonjudgmental, compassionate medical care for wounds they inflict on themselves, care that does not rob them of their dignity or autonomy. Together, client and therapist can devise a plan for getting physical wounds treated without contributing additional stress to the situation. This may involve educating physicians at local emergency rooms about the nature of self-injury.

Therapy can be very helpful to a person trying to get past self-injury. It is important that the patient trust the therapist, and that the therapist understand the problems that lie at the heart of the patient's behavior.

Since successful treatment of self-injury depends heavily on teaching the client new ways of coping with pain or stress, hospitalization should be used only as a last resort, when the client is at risk for suicide or severe permanent self-inflicted injury. Hospitals are artificially safe environments, and the necessary tasks of learning to identify the feelings behind the act and of choosing a less destructive method of coping need to be practiced and reinforced in the real world.

A patient who self-mutilates may be allowed to contact her therapist at any time, but restricted from contact for a period of time if she harms herself. This forces the patient to decide whether or not self-mutilation is worth the negative consequences.

DIALECTICAL BEHAVIORAL THERAPY

One way that self-injurious behavior is treated is dialectical behavioral therapy (DBT). Used in combination with traditional *psychotherapy* (therapist intervention to modify behavior) and *pharmacotherapy* (drug-related treatments) to control the condition, DBT attempts to change the patient's social behavior. This is called a *psychosocial* element of the treatment.

Basically, DBT maintains that some people react abnormally to emotional stimulation. Their level of arousal goes up much more quickly, peaks at a higher level, and takes more time to settle. This may be caused by invalidating environments during childhood, or it may be the result of unknown biological factors. However, in theory the people in this situation have not developed ways to cope with sudden, intense surges of emotion, perhaps because of their past invalidation, and they may have extremely unstable emotions and chaotic lives. DBT helps teach the coping skills these people need.

The primary goal of DBT is to reduce self-injuring and life-threatening behaviors. Another goal is to minimize behavior that either interferes with the therapy/treatment process or diminishes the client's quality of life. The emphasis is on teaching patients how to manage emotional trauma, rather than on taking them out of crises.

DBT targets behaviors in a descending hierarchy:

1. Decrease high-risk suicidal behaviors
2. Decrease responses or behaviors (by either the therapist or the patient) that interfere with therapy
3. Decrease behaviors that interfere with/reduce quality of life
4. Decrease and deal with post-traumatic stress responses
5. Enhance respect for self
6. Acquire behavioral skills
7. Achieve additional goals set by the patient

There are two therapy elements to DBT: a weekly one-on-one meeting with a psychiatrist, and a weekly group therapy session. At the weekly psychotherapy session, doctor and patient explore in detail a particular behavior or event from the past week. They begin by discussing how the situation developed, then they review various solutions that might have been used to resolve the problem, and examine how the client responded. Between sessions the patient is encouraged to stay in touch with the therapist by telephone so that adaptive behaviors can be reinforced. The group therapy sessions, each typically about two and a half hours long, teach coping skills. These include interpersonal effectiveness (ways of working

In combination with one-on-one therapeutic treatment, group therapy is usually helpful. Two types of therapy are common: dialectical behavioral therapy and interpersonal group therapy.

more effectively with other people); distress tolerance (learning how to face and deal with stressful situations); reality acceptance skills; and emotion regulation. Group therapists are not available over the phone between sessions; they refer patients in crisis to the individual therapist.

INTERPERSONAL GROUP THERAPY

Although on the surface interpersonal group therapy (IGT) seems to share many elements with DBT, the two treatment methodologies are extremely different. IGT therapists don't take a one-on-one teaching approach at all. This form of therapy involves group sessions, where each member of the group describes a social situation he or she faced in the past week and how he or she dealt with it. The members of the group discuss each situation and share ways to deal with frustration or problems. An acceptable response for each situation is worked out within the group by the patients, with the therapist intervening only when the process of therapy seems to be getting off track (this is called *derailing*).

Therapist interventions in IGT are intended to be tentative, exploratory, indirect, and neutral. The therapist may answer questions or make supportive statements, or, if the discussion is proceeding in the wrong direction, may express doubt or confusion over group members' opinions. Another method the therapist can use to guide the discussion is reiteration or paraphrasing, in which a statement is repeated in different words so the listener is sure he or she understands.

Some patients have said they feel "safe" with interpersonal group therapy because the group sessions are structured—they are held at a fixed date and time, and for a specific length of time. Clinicians and therapists feel this structure has particular therapeutic value, because the patients have had repeated experiences with unpredictable or unsafe interpersonal encounters.

SCARS

For some people scars aren't an issue–they self-injure in ways that don't leave permanent marks, or they only injure in places that are normally covered by clothing (the torso, shoulders, and so on). For most people who cut or burn, though, scars are a major problem.

Sometimes it's possible to hide scars. Wrist scars can be covered by long sleeves, bracelets, or watches. Some leg scars on women can be hidden by panty hose or tights. Heavy concealer makeup can be used to hide faint scars. For some types of scarring, special creams or bandages may help. Plastic surgery might be effective for some kinds of scarring, but it is very expensive and often leaves scars of its own.

RATIONAL-EMOTIVE THERAPY

Rational-emotive therapy (RET) is a form of cognitive therapy; cognitive therapists seek to change a person's thoughts, feelings, and behaviors. This, these doctors believe, should lead to more agreeable behavior and an improved quality of life for the patient. The precepts of rational-emotive therapy can be helpful in controlling the sometimes uncontrollable rage self-injurers feel.

RET was developed in the 1960s by a doctor named Albert Ellis. He believed that feelings don't control thoughts—thoughts control feelings. Negative emotions are not inevitable, but come about as the result of patterns of thinking we've laid down over the years. If a person can learn to rethink the situations, that person can learn to control his or her angry or negative emotions.

The following story is an example of how rational-emotive therapy can help a person to defuse anger or frustration:

> Fred was working on an important paper for his high school English class when his younger brother tripped on the computer cord, pulling it from the wall socket. This shut the machine down, and Fred's unsaved paper was lost. He would have to redo all the work.
>
> Fred's first thoughts were, "Why did he have to do that? Couldn't he see I was working? He should look where he's going, and he shouldn't even come around when I'm working anyway." Fred became angry and his initial response was to yell at his brother and blame him for the lost work. But remembering the discussions about anger he had had with his therapist, Fred took a moment to reconsider, and question, his reaction.
>
> "Accidents happen," Fred told himself. "It's not like he did it on purpose. It'd be nice if he didn't rush through the room when I'm working, but I can deal with that."
>
> Fred decided that in the future he'd like to have less risk of having his work interrupted and lost by unexpected intrusions, without making his brother angry or being unrealistic. Although he was still upset—using RET techniques does not eliminate feelings—he was feeling only frustrated and disappointed, not enraged.
>
> Instead of taking out his frustration on his little brother, Fred decided to respond to the situation constructively. He looked around and decided that he could move the computer cord, to make

One way that psychologists seek to help a person eliminate angry feelings is through rational-emotive therapy (RET). The precepts of rational-emotive therapy can be helpful in controlling the sometimes uncontrollable rage self-injurers feel.

it harder to accidentally unplug. He also decided to save his work more often. In the future these two changes might help prevent the problem he was faced with now. Fred moved the computer cord and set his word processing program to automatically save documents every three minutes.

In this example, it is not easy for Fred to control his anger. In real life it is rarely easy, either. But through continued meetings and discussion with the therapist, patients can learn to control their negative feelings and use them for positive accomplishments.

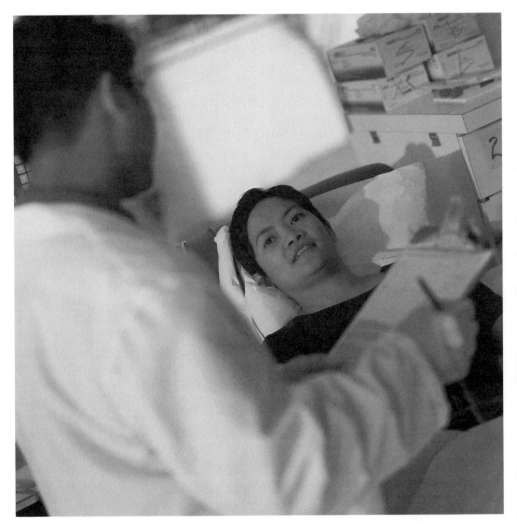

Hospital treatment for people who self-mutilate is usually only done as a last resort.

HOSPITAL-BASED TREATMENT

As mentioned earlier in this chapter, hospital-based treatment is usually done only as a last resort. Hospital-based treatment may be done on either an inpatient basis (the client is admitted to the hospital) or an outpatient basis (the client comes to the hospital or clinic for treatment, but lives at home). One hospital program that has been successful is Safe Alternatives (1-800-DONTCUT), an inpatient program specifically for self-injurers that is located at McNeal Hospital in suburban Chicago. The program combines various therapy techniques as well as group and individual exercises to help patients gain an awareness of why they hurt themselves and how to stop.

Although there is no shortage of theories about why people hurt themselves, each of the forms of therapy discussed in this chapter has been effective in helping people to control self-harming behavior. The important thing for people who self-mutilate is to find a therapist they can work with and trust. They should ask a prospective therapist about his or her views on self-injury—why people do it, how the doctor will approach it therapeutically, and what outcome to expect—and make sure that the answers are ones with which they feel comfortable.

Self-help or support groups can be helpful, especially organizations geared specifically toward people who self-injure. Crisis lines, women's resource centers, and rape or sexual abuse organizations may also be sources of information about such groups in your area.

If you cut or harm yourself, it can be difficult to tell others about this self-injury.

5

HELPING YOURSELF STOP SELF-INJURY

I t is very personal, and can be very difficult, when you decide to stop injuring yourself. You may have to consider your situation for a long time
before deciding that you are ready to commit to a life without scars and
bruises. Don't be discouraged if you conclude the time isn't right for you to
stop yet; you can still exert more control over your self-injury by choosing
when and how much you harm yourself, by setting limits for your self-harm,
and by taking responsibility for it. If you choose to do this, you should take
care to remain safe when harming yourself: don't share cutting implements
and know basic first aid for treating your injuries.

DELAYING THE ACT:
THE FIRST STEP TO RECOVERY

When you feel the urge to injure yourself, try to delay the act in any way
you can. Dr. Armando Favazza calls the willingness and ability to delay self-
injury the first step to recovery. You might try distracting yourself by call-
ing a friend, going somewhere, writing in a journal, watching a movie,
painting a picture, exercising, or doing some other diverting task. Even if
you fear that waiting will cause you to hurt yourself worse, try to hold off.
Quitting self-mutilation is like quitting alcohol or drugs; many people find
that the longer they go without harming themselves, the easier it becomes
to resist.

It may be helpful to stay in the company of others. People usually injure
themselves privately. Spend as much time as possible in public places, or stay
overnight with a trusted friend or family member. Some people find that the
impulse to injure themselves passes if a loved one holds them tightly when
they are feeling overwhelmed by their feelings or out of touch with their
bodies. Some people find it helpful to say "No!" or "Stop!" out loud when

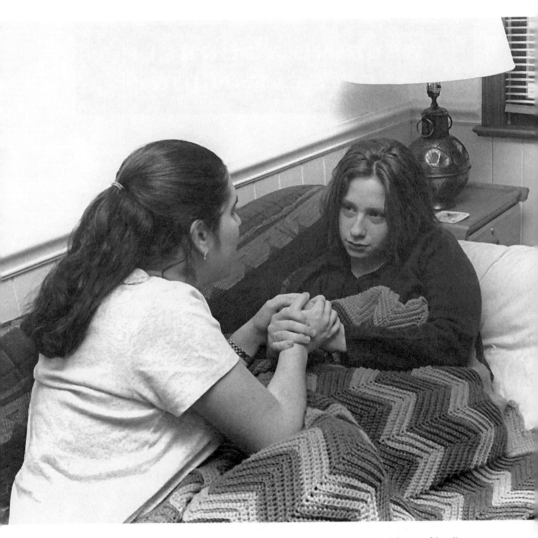

If you feel the urge to self-mutilate, it may be helpful to spend the night at a friend's house. This may help you delay the need to cut or hurt yourself—the first step to recovery.

they think of hurting themselves. This seems to interrupt the immediate need to self-injure in response to stress.

When the urge comes, avoid materials that you might hurt yourself with, like razors, glass, pins, cigarette lighters, or knives. In the short term many people find it helpful to remove razor blades or other tempting items from their home. If you can, give them to a person you trust, who knows that you have been harming yourself, and ask that person to help keep you from getting more. You should also stay away from drugs and alcohol, as these can contribute to the feelings that prompt self-mutilation.

If these strategies fail, remind yourself about the long-term consequences of self-injury—scars and permanent physical damage or social rejection being a few possibilities.

ALTERNATIVE WAYS OF DEALING WITH PROBLEMS

Several different strategies are typically suggested for dealing with a crisis: squeezing ice, taking a cold bath or a hot or cold shower, biting into something strongly flavored (hot peppers; ginger root; unpeeled lemon, lime, or grapefruit), rubbing a medicated ointment under your nose, and so on. A strong taste or smell may provide your body with the shock it needs to overcome the urge to cut.

These strategies work because the intense emotions that provoke self-injury are passing; they come and go like waves, and if you can stay upright through one, you get some breathing room before the next. The more waves you can withstand without falling over, the stronger you become.

Aren't these things just the same as punishing yourself by cutting or burning or hitting or whatever? The key difference is that they don't produce lasting results. If you squeeze a handful of ice until it melts, or stick a couple of fingers into some ice cream for a few minutes, it'll hurt but it won't leave scars. It won't leave anything you'll have to explain away later, and you most likely won't feel guilty afterward.

These kinds of distractions won't cure the roots of your self-injury, but they will help you get through an intense moment without making things worse for yourself in the long run. They're training wheels, and they teach you that you can get through a crisis without hurting yourself. You will refine them, even devise more productive coping mechanisms later, as the urge to self-injure lessens and loses the hold it has on your life. Use these methods to demonstrate to yourself that you can cope with distress without permanently injuring your body. Every

People usually injure themselves privately, so spending time with others is a good way to distract yourself from the need to self-injure.

time you do, you make self-injury that much less likely next time you're in crisis.

USING NEW COPING STRATEGIES

Your first task when you've decided to stop is to break the cycle, to force yourself to try new coping mechanisms. And you do have to force yourself to do this; it doesn't just happen. You can't theorize about new coping techniques until one day they're all in place and your life is changed. You have to work, to struggle, to make yourself behave differently.

When you pick up that knife or that lighter, or get ready to hit that wall, you must make a conscious decision to do something else. At first the something else will be very basic, maybe even punishing, and that's okay—the important thing is that you make the decision not to hurt yourself. This is a moment of mastery: you decide that you are not going to injure yourself. This makes your self-injury a choice.

Before you cut or harm yourself, take a few moments to look behind the urge. What are you feeling? Are you angry? Frustrated? Restless? Sad? Craving the feeling of self-injury? Do you feel depersonalized and unreal or numb? Unfocused? When you know why you want to hurt yourself, try to find something else to do that will allow you to vent your frustrations in a safe way.

If you are angry or frustrated, do something that is physical and violent but not directed at a living thing. Instead of cutting yourself, slash an empty plastic soda bottle, a piece of heavy cardboard, or an old shirt or sock. Sometime when you are not feeling upset or depressed, you could even make a soft cloth doll or small clay figures to represent the things you are angry about; then when you are angry, cut and tear at the doll or smash the figures instead of hurting yourself. Another alternative is to take a drawing or photo of yourself and mark in red ink what you want to do to ease your painful feelings, instead of actually cutting or hurting yourself. To blow off steam you could flatten aluminum cans for recycling, seeing how fast you can go; hit a punching bag; hit a wall with a pillow; rip up an old newspaper or phone book; break sticks or wooden dowels; or stomp around in heavy shoes. You could also divert your feelings into positive channels—clean your room (or your whole house); go for a walk, jog, or run; play a sport like handball or tennis; or just crank up the music and dance.

If you are feeling sad, melancholy, or depressed, do something slow and soothing, like taking a hot bath with bath oil or bubbles, or curling up under a comforter with hot cocoa and a good book. Light sweet-smelling incense, listen to soothing music, and rub a nice body lotion into the parts of yourself you want to hurt. Call or visit a friend and just talk about things that you like, or make a tray of special treats and tuck yourself into bed with them to read or watch television. In short, do whatever makes you feel taken care of and comforted.

Activities like in-line skating can be positive outlets for feelings of anger or frustration—a much better alternative to self-mutilation.

If you find that you are craving sensation, feeling depersonalized, dissociated, or unreal, do something that creates a sharp physical sensation. Take several pieces of ice and squeeze them as hard as you can. This really hurts, but will not leave permanent damage. Putting ice on a spot you want to burn gives you a powerful, painful sensation and leaves a red mark afterward, kind of like burning would. Some other ways to create a strong sensation might include biting into a hot pepper or chewing a piece of ginger root, rubbing liniment under your nose, slapping a tabletop hard, snapping your wrist with a rubber band, or taking a cold bath.

If you feel the problem is that you lack focus, do a task that is exacting and requires concentration. Choose an object in the room, examine it carefully, and then write as detailed a description of it as you can. Include everything: size, weight, texture, shape, color, and possible uses. You could also select a random object, like a paper clip, and try to list 30 different uses for it.

If your strong feeling is to see blood, draw on yourself with a red felt-tip pen. Or take a small bottle of red food coloring and warm it slightly by dropping it into a cup of hot water for a few minutes. Uncap the bottle and press its tip against the place you want to cut. Draw the bottle in a cutting motion while squeezing it slightly to let the food coloring trickle out. Or paint yourself with red tempera paint. If you want to see scars or pick scabs, get a henna tattoo kit. You put the henna on as a paste and leave it overnight; the next day you can pick it off as you would a scab, and it leaves an orange red mark behind.

Another thing that helps sometimes is the fifteen-minute game. Tell yourself that if you still want to harm yourself in 15 minutes, you can. When the time is up, see if you can go for another 15 minutes.

THINKING ABOUT SELF-MUTILATION

It's not uncommon for people who self-mutilate to continue thinking obsessively about injuring themselves after they've made the decision to stop. Hurting themselves has been an important aspect of their life up to that decision, so thoughts about it will not magically vanish from their head. Even though the decision to stop self-injuring is a step toward healing, it alone is not a cure for the person's problems.

If you are a person who self-injures and have made the decision to stop, don't become frustrated when you catch yourself thinking

If you feel you cannot focus, do something that requires concentration, such as playing a musical instrument.

about cutting or harming yourself, and don't despair that you will never be able to end your self-destructive feelings.

One way to cope with the feelings is to designate two 10- or 15-minute time periods each day. Choose times when you will be alone and will be able to think without being interrupted. During those times allow yourself to obsess about hurting yourself. Think about what it would feel like, how you would feel afterward, how much you want to do it—all those thoughts you've been trying to suppress. Get as distressed as you can and stay focused on the topic of injuring yourself. You may find, especially after the first few times, that you get really bored toward the end of your time period. That's a good sign—you're accepting the change in your lifestyle.

When the time is up, stop thinking about self-injury. If thoughts of wanting to harm come into your mind at other times during the day, acknowledge them and remind yourself that you will think about them later, when it's time. Then let them go. If they come back, repeat the process. Don't try to ignore them; just acknowledge them, remind yourself they have their time soon, and let go. Most people notice an improvement after a week or so, some after just a few days.

One crucial thing: no matter what, do not act on the thoughts of self-injury. They are just thoughts, and you can use the skills discussed in this chapter, such as distraction and substitution, to get through these times.

WHEN NOTHING ELSE WORKS

Sometimes you will make a good-faith effort to keep from harming yourself, but nothing seems to work. You've slashed a bottle, your hand is numb from crushing ice, and the urge to cut or burn yourself is still twisting your insides into knots. You feel that if you don't harm yourself, you'll explode. What now?

Before you take that step, take a few minutes to ask yourself the questions below. Answer them as honestly and in as much detail as you can. No one will know the answers but you, and there is no reason to lie to yourself.

1. Why do I feel I need to hurt myself? What has brought me to this point?

2. Have I been here before? What did I do to deal with it? How did I feel then?

3. What I have done to ease this discomfort so far? What else can I do that won't hurt me?

4. How do I feel right now?

5. How will I feel when I am hurting myself?

6. How will I feel after hurting myself? How will I feel tomorrow morning?

7. Can I avoid this stressor or deal with it better in the future?

8. Do I need to hurt myself?

Just answering these questions may help you to decide that you do not want or need to hurt yourself. However, if you have tried all the coping strategies, reminded yourself about the consequences of self-injury, and hung on as long as you could but still feel the overwhelming urge to harm yourself, don't get discouraged. Self-mutilation is a very hard behavior to change. Try to focus on longer-term methods to decrease your stress, finding new ways to communicate and express your feelings, or increasing your control over self-harm instead of dwelling on the fact that you hurt yourself again.

TELLING PEOPLE ABOUT YOUR SELF-INJURY

Self-injury is not something that can be tucked away in a little corner of a person's life where it doesn't touch anything else. Even after a person has stopped self-mutilation, it continues to affect who he or she is and how he or she interacts with people. Scars fade but never disappear entirely. Feelings of alienation may subside but still lurk in the background.

It can be very difficult to admit to family and friends that you self-injure, just as it would be difficult to admit a substance-abuse problem or infection with a disease such as AIDS. Most people assume that they should tell others about their self-injury in a face-to-face conversation, but that's not the only way to present this news. Some people have found that writing down everything they want to say and presenting it to their family member, partner, or friend has worked for them. Do whatever makes you feel most comfortable, but be sensitive to the other person's feelings. It can be nearly as hard for them to hear about your self-mutilation as it is for you to tell them about it.

When you are ready, choose a place that is private and a time when the person or people you want to tell are available for a long conversation, if you wish to tell them face-to-face. If you're rushed or afraid that other people nearby will overhear what you are talking about and react, you're not going to be able to give your full attention to the conversation and neither will anyone else. You may want to consider asking a friend or therapist who understands your situation to sit in on the conversation. A neutral third person can help keep things calm.

As you discuss your situation, explain that "coming out" is an act of love. Let them know that your deciding to tell them about self-injury

It can be very difficult to tell someone that you self-mutilate; it can also be very hard for that friend or loved one to hear about it. When you do decide to talk to someone about your need to cut or harm yourself, select a person that you can trust and who will understand what you have been going through.

is a sign of your love for and trust in them. The desire to be open and trust them outweighs the fear of rejection or hatred or disgust. Let the people you're "coming out" to know you're not trying to punish them, manipulate them, or make them feel guilty.

It's not necessary to bring up the most disturbing topics in the first conversation. In fact, it is probably best to avoid graphic descriptions of what you do. However, you should provide as much information as you can and answer any questions openly and honestly. Many people

ARE YOU READY TO STOP HURTING YOURSELF?

I f you are a person who self-injures, ask yourself the following checklist of questions when you are ready to stop cutting or harming yourself. The more "yes" answers you can give to these questions, the easier it will be to stop hurting yourself.

- Do I want to stop hurting myself?

- Do I have a solid emotional support system of friends, family, and/or professionals I trust who can help me if I feel like hurting myself? Anytime I feel the need to self-injure, are there at least two people I can call?

- Do I feel at least somewhat comfortable talking about my self-injury with three different people?

- Have I made a list of at least 10 things I can do instead of hurting myself?

- Do I have a place to go if I need to leave my house so as not to hurt myself?

- Do I feel confident that I could get rid of all the things that I might be likely to use to hurt myself (razors, scissors, cigarettes, knives, etc.)?

- Have I told at least two other people that I am going to stop hurting myself?

- Am I willing to feel uncomfortable, scared, and frustrated, because I realize that these are feelings all people share and that injuring myself to avoid them is not the answer?

- Can I think about hurting myself without actually having to do so?

have never heard of self-injury or do not understand it. Be prepared to answer their questions about self-injury, and encourage them to ask. You might want to anticipate potential questions to get an idea of how you want to respond. It is quite possible that one of the questions will be about what you want to do about your self-mutilation. They may ask if you want treatment, how it can be treated, if you want them to help you stop, and how they can help. The important thing is to communicate and be as open as you can. The more people know about something, the less they fear it.

You should never use your self-injury as a weapon: "You made me cut/burn/scratch/hit!" Whether or not they have contributed to the problems that led to your self-injury is irrelevant to this initial conversation. If you start getting angry and placing blame, you're going to put the other person or people on the defensive and they'll get angry. Using self-injury as a weapon also increases the likelihood that the person you're "coming out" to will react in exactly the ways you're hoping they won't. The causes of your self-injury can be discussed later, once all the people involved understand what is happening.

Be willing to give the other people some time to digest, though—if you follow up with them and they say, "I'd like to think about this for a while," give them space. Ask them to let you know when they're ready to talk, and let it go.

If a friend tells you that she self-mutilates, it is important to be accepting and supportive. Try to make your friend feel safe discussing her self-harming behavior, and don't be judgmental.

6

HELPING SOMEONE
WHO SELF-INJURES

At some time you might learn that a friend or loved one has been cutting or harming himself or herself. Perhaps someone you care about trusts you enough to tell you about his or her self-injury, or maybe you've discovered it inadvertently. Regardless of how you found out, you know about the situation, and even though it may be difficult to understand or to deal with, you can't pretend it will go away—you must respond in some way.

It is important to maintain an accepting, open attitude about the person who self-mutilates. In many cases the person will have a problem with self-esteem or may be upset or embarrassed by the self-injurious behavior. Try to make the person feel safe discussing it and feel accepted regardless of his or her behavior. Try not to pay more attention to the cutting or self-harming behavior than to the healthier things that this person does, and don't make judgmental statements about the self-injury. Even if you say something only once, the person may remember it for months or even years. Be helpful and understanding, not dismissive. This chapter provides some guidelines for helping and coping with a friend or family member who self-injures.

BEING SUPPORTIVE

Don't avoid the subject of self-injury. Let it be known that you're willing to talk, and then follow the other person's lead. For example, you might say to your girlfriend, "I know that sometimes you hurt yourself, and I'd like to understand it. People do it for so many reasons; if you could help me understand yours, I'd be grateful." Don't push it after that; if the person says she'd rather not talk about it, drop the subject, perhaps reminding her that you're willing to listen if she ever does want to talk about it. Tell the person that if you don't bring the subject up, it's because you're respecting her space, not because it upsets or bothers you. Some people need time to decide to trust someone

Provide distractions for a friend who is troubled: take a walk, talk about a good book, or share some ice cream. Even if your friend is not ready to talk about problems, knowing that you are there will help.

else, particularly if they've received a lot of negative feedback about their self-injury before. Be patient.

If the person is not ready to talk about her problem, or is not ready to deal with what she is doing, you can help by providing distractions. For a person who is feeling depressed or upset, sometimes just having someone to do something with—to go to a movie, on a walk, or out for ice cream—can work wonders. If the person you're concerned about does not live with you, offer safe physical space: "I'm worried about you; Would you come sleep over at my house tonight?" Even if the offer is declined, just knowing you were concerned and wanted to help can be comforting. Also, don't ask, "Is there anything I can do?"; instead, find things that you can do, and then ask, "Do you mind if I . . ." People who feel really bad often can't think of anything that might make them feel better; asking if you can take them to a movie or talk about something not related to their self-mutilation can be really helpful.

This doesn't mean that you should ignore your friend's or loved one's feelings; you can acknowledge that she feels lousy and still do something nice or distracting. Don't try to cajole the person out of her depressed mood or tell her to just "get over it"—you should just try to lift her spirits by offering something positive. Don't expect your efforts to be a permanent cure, though; they are simply a technique to improve the moment and, hopefully, help the person feel better without harming herself.

If you think your friend or loved one is in immediate danger of cutting or other superficial or moderate self-injury, stay with her until the impulse passes, or encourage her not to be alone. Physical contact through hand holding or hugging can sometimes be helpful if the relationship is appropriate and trust is sufficient.

When your friend or family member is willing to share information about her self-injurious behavior, be supportive without reinforcing the behavior. Don't browbeat the person if she fails at controlling the self-injury, and praise any success that she has in delaying or avoiding the act. It's important that the person knows that you can separate who she is from what she does, and that you love her no matter what. Be available as much as you can be. Set aside your personal feelings of fear or revulsion about the behavior and focus on what's going on with the person.

Ultimatums do not work—ever. No matter how much you care about someone, you cannot force her to behave as you'd prefer. Punishing a person for her self-injurious behavior, or making her feel guilty about it, just continues the cycle of self-hatred and frustration that leads to self-injury. Confiscating tools used for self-injury is worse than useless—it just encourages the person to be creative in finding new ways to cut or hurt herself. Rather than saying, "I will stop loving you if you cut yourself," say, "I cannot handle talking to you while you are actually cutting yourself, because I care about you greatly and it hurts too much to see you doing that." Make it clear from your behavior that the person doesn't need to self-injure in order to get displays of love and caring from you. Be free with loving, caring gestures, even if they aren't always (or even often) returned. Don't withdraw your love from the person. The way to avoid reinforcing self-injury is to be consistently caring, so that taking care of the person after she injures is nothing special or extraordinary.

Though you should be understanding, it is also essential that you recognize the severity of your friend or loved one's distress and inability to stop cutting. Try not to get angry at her injurious behavior, because this merely reinforces the negative feelings that led to the behavior in the first place. Also, don't minimize how much distress the person is feeling by making statements like "It's not that bad" or "You can't be that upset about it." Be supportive: acknowledge that the person is under a lot of stress and explain that you are there if there's anything you can do to help. Acknowledging and accepting that someone is in pain doesn't make the pain go away, but it can make it more bearable. Let your friend know you understand that self-injury isn't an attempt to be willful or to make life hard or unpleasant for you; acknowledge that it's caused by genuine pain she can find no other way to handle.

Part of being supportive is trying to help your friend or family member resolve the problems that led her to self-mutilate. If she is open to it, discuss possibilities for treatment. Encourage her, if she is not already doing so, to find a professional therapist who meets her needs, preferably one who has knowledge of and experience with repetitive self-injury. Also, you can participate with your friend in self-injury support groups, if they exist in your area.

Overcoming self-injury can be a long and difficult process for both the patient and for those who love her. Support from family and friends makes it easier to end the cycle of deliberate self-harm.

COPING WITH THE PROBLEM

Self-injury is an extremely stressful, frustrating, and anxiety-provoking situation—for everyone involved. Though it is important to be supportive, do not neglect your own feelings or mental state. Be honest with yourself about how this person's self-mutilation makes you feel. Don't try to pretend that you're not bothered if, in fact, you are—many people find self-injury repulsive or frightening.

If you need help dealing with the feelings self-injury arouses in you, find a good therapist, preferably one with knowledge of and experience with treating self-mutilation. You should not see the same therapist who is treating your friend or loved one, however. Be careful that you don't try to use your therapy to help your friend or family member—what goes on in your therapy sessions should remain between you and your therapist. Don't discuss the content of your therapy sessions in any but the most general terms, and never say anything like "My therapist says you should . . ." Therapy is a tool for self-understanding, not for getting others to change.

Most importantly, don't take your friend or loved one's self-harming behavior personally. The person you're concerned about is not cutting, burning, or harming herself just to make you feel bad or guilty. Even if her actions feel like manipulation, they probably aren't intended as such. People generally do not self-injure to be dramatic, to annoy others, or to make a point; in fact, they often don't even realize how much their behavior upsets others besides themselves.

Taking care of yourself can be hard work. If you constantly try to be completely supportive to someone, you're going to burn out; this won't help your friend or loved one. Remember that as much as you love this person, sometimes you're going to need to get away from her for a while. Take a break from the situation when you need to, and set clear limits on what you will do to help. Tell the person that sometimes you need to recharge, and that it doesn't affect your love for her. Break into this personal time only in cases of absolute life-or-death crisis.

You have to be sure your own needs are being met. The balance here is tricky, because if you make yourself more and more distant, you might get a reaction of increasing levels of crisis from the other person. If you let her know that she doesn't have to be on the verge of death to get love and attention from you, you can take breaks more easily. The key is developing trust, a process that will take some time. Once you prove that you are someone who isn't going to go away at the first sign of trouble, you will be able to go away in non-crisis times without provoking a problem.

Although overcoming self-injury can be a long and difficult process for both the patients and for those who love them, it is important to remember that people who are strong enough to survive the abuse or trauma that led to self-injury are also strong enough to stop hurting themselves.

APPENDIX

FOR MORE INFORMATION

**Adolescent Psychiatric Services
at Fairfax Hospital**
10200 N.E. 132nd Street
Kirkland, Washington 98034
Phone: (800) 435-7221
Fax: (425) 821-9010
Website: http://athealth.com/fairfax.html

Butler Hospital
345 Blackstone Boulevard
Providence, RI 02906
Phone: (401) 455-6200
Website: http://www.butler.org

The Cutting Edge (newsletter)
PO Box 20819
Cleveland, OH 44120

Frederick County Mental Health Association
357-359 W. Patrick Street
Frederick, MD 21701
Phone: (301) 663-6135
24-hour Hotline: (301) 662-2255
Website: http://www.fwp.net/Mental
  HealthAssoc/counhot.htm

**Independent Living Center
of the North Shore**
583 Chestnut Street
Lynn, MA 01904
Phone: (617) 593-7500
Publishes the pamphlet "Women and
  Self Injury" and offers support groups.

**Institute for Bio-behavioral Therapy
and Research**
935 Northern Boulevard
Great Neck, NY 11021
Phone: (516) 487-7116
Website: http://www.babyplace.com/
  biobehav.htm

Linehan Training Group
4556 University Way NE
College Center Building, Suite 222
Seattle, WA 98105
E-mail: info@dbt-seattle.com

Pittsburgh Action Against Rape (PAAR)
81 S. 19th Street
Pittsburgh, PA 15203
Phone: (412) 431-5665
Website: http://drewski.andrew.cmu.
  edu/survivors/selfinjury

SAFE Alternatives Program
MacNeal Hospital
Berwyn, IL
Hotline: (800) DONT CUT

The Sanctuary
Friends Hospital
4641 Roosevelt Boulevard
Philadelphia, PA 19124-2399
Phone: (215) 831-6916
Website: http://www.sanctuarysage.com

APPENDIX

BIBLIOGRAPHY

Barnes, R. "Women and Self-Injury." *International Journal of Women's Studies* 8, no. 5 (May 1985): 465–475.

Bottsworth, Loralei, and Stephanie Pedersen. "Making the Cut." *Teen Magazine*, March 1998.

Brodsky, Beth S., Marylene Cloitre, and Rebecca A. Dulit. "Relationship of Dissociation to Self-Mutilation and Childhood Abuse in Borderline Personality Disorder." *American Journal of Psychiatry* 152, no. 12 (December 1995).

DiClemente, R. L. Ponton, and D. Hartley. "Prevalence and Correlates of Cutting Behavior: Risk for HIV Transmission." *Journal of the American Academy of Child and Adolescent Psychiatry* 30, no. 5 (May 1991): 735–739.

Dulit, Rebecca A., Minna R. Fyer, Andrew C. Leon, Beth S. Brodsky, and Allen J. Frances. "Clinical Correlates of Self-Mutilation in Borderline Personality Disorder." *American Journal of Psychiatry* 151, no. 9 (September 1994).

Egan, Jennifer. "The Thin Red Line." *The New York Times Magazine,* July 27, 1997.

Favazza, Armando R. *Bodies Under Siege: Self-Mutilation and Body Modification in Culture and Psychiatry,* 2nd ed. Baltimore: The Johns Hopkins University Press, 1996.

———. "Why Patients Mutilate Themselves." *Hospital and Community Psychiatry* 40, no. 2 (1989): 137–145.

Favazza, Armando R., and K. Conterio. "The Plight of Chronic Self-Mutilators." *Community Mental Health Journal* 24, no. 8 (August 1988): 22–30.

———. "Self-Mutilation and Eating Disorders." *Suicide and Life Threatening Behavior* (Fall 1988).

Favazza, Armando R., and R. J. Rosenthal. "Diagnostic Issues in Self-Mutilation." *Hospital and Community Psychiatry* 44, no. 2 (1993): 134–140.

Golden, B., and J. Walker-O'Keefe. "Self-Injury: Hidden Pain in the Workplace." *EAP Digest* 13, no. 6 (November/December 1986): 68–69.

Greenspan, G.S., and S.E. Samuel. "Self-Cutting After Rape." *American Journal of Psychiatry* 146 (1989): 789–790.

Gunderson, John G., and Paul Links. "Borderline Personality Disorder" *Treatments of Psychiatric Disorders*, 2nd ed. Washington D.C.: American Psychiatric Press, 1994.

Herman, John, J. C. Perry, and B. Van der Kolk. "Childhood Trauma in Borderline Personality Disorder." *American Journal of Psychiatry* 146 (1989): 490–495.

Kahan, J., and E. M. Pattison. "The Deliberate Self-Harm Syndrome." *American Journal of Psychiatry* 140 (1983): 867–872.

———. "Proposal for a Distinctive Diagnosis: The Deliberate Self-Harm Syndrome." *Suicide and Life Threatening Behavior* 14 (1984): 17–35.

Landecker, H. "The Role of Childhood Sexual Trauma in the Etiology of Borderline Personality Disorder: Considerations for Diagnosis and Treatment." *Psychotherapy* 29 (1992): 234–42.

Linehan, Marsha M., Darren A. Tutek, Heidi L. Heard, and Hubert E. Armstrong. "Interpersonal Outcome of Cognitive Behavioral Treatment for Chronically Suicidal Borderline Patients." *American Journal of Psychiatry* 151, no. 12 (December 1994): 1771–75.

Linehan, M. M., H. Armstrong, et al. "Cognitive-Behavioral Treatment of Chronically Parasuicidal Borderline Patients." *Archives of General Psychiatry* 48 (1991): 1060–1064.

Malinosky-Rummel, R. and D. J. Hanson. "Long-Term Consequences of Childhood Physical Abuse." *Psychology Bulletin* 114 (1993): 68–79.

Malon, D. W., and D. Bnerardi. "Hyponsis with Self-Cutters." *American Journal of Psychotherapy* 50, no. 4 (April 1987): 531–541.

Richardson, J. S., and W. A. Zaleski. "Endogenous Opiates and Self-Mutilation." *American Journal of Psychiatry* 140 (1983): 938–939.

Simeon, Daphne, Barbara Stanley, Allen Frances, J. John Mann, Ronald Winchel, and Michael Stanley. "Self-Mutilation in Personality Disorders: Psychological and Biological Correlates." *American Journal of Psychiatry* 149, no. 2 (February 1992).

Todd, Andrea. "Razor's Edge." *Seventeen Magazine*, June 1996.

Winchel, R. M., and M. Stanley. "Self-Injurious Behavior: A Review of the Behavior and Biology of Self-Mutilation." *American Journal of Psychiatry* 148, no. 3 (March 1991): 306–315.

Yaryura-Tobias, J. A., F. A. Neziroglu, and S. Kaplan. "Self-Mutilation, Anorexia, and Dysmenorrhea in Obsessive Compulsive Disorder." *International Journal of Eating Disorders* 17, no. 1 (January 1995): 33–38.

APPENDIX

FURTHER READING

Alderman, Tracy. *The Scarred Soul: Understanding and Ending Self-Inflicted Violence.* Oakland: New Harbinger, 1997.

American Psychiatric Association. *Diagnostic and Statistical Manual of Mental Disorders,* 4th ed. Washington, D.C.: American Psychiatric Press, 1994.

———. *Treatment of Psychiatric Disorders,* 2nd ed. 2 vols. Washington, D.C.: American Psychiatric Press, 1994.

Cronkite, Kay. *On the Edge of Darkness: Conversations about Conquering Depression.* New York: W. W. Norton, 1995.

Favazza, A. R. *Bodies Under Siege: Self-Mutilation and Body Modification in Culture and Psychiatry,* 2nd ed. Baltimore: The Johns Hopkins University Press, 1996.

Gabbard, Glen O., Susan G. Lazar, John Hornberger, and David Spiegel. "The Economic Impact of Psychotherapy: A Review." *American Journal of Psychiatry* 154, no. 2 (February 1997).

Kernberg, O. F. *Severe Personality Disorders: Psychotherapeutic Strategies.* New Haven: Yale University Press, 1986.

Kubetin, C., and J. D. Mallory. *Beyond the Darkness.* Dallas: Word/Rapha, 1992.

Levenkron, S. *The Luckiest Girl in the World.* New York: Scribner, 1997.

———. *Cutting: Understanding and Overcoming Self-Mutilation.* New York: W. W. Norton, 1998.

Linehan, M. M. *Cognitive-Behavioral Treatment of Borderline Personality Disorder.* New York: The Guilford Press, 1993.

———. *Skills Training Manual for Treating Borderline Personality Disorder.* New York: The Guilford Press, 1993.

Luiselli, J. K., J. L. Matson, and N. N. Singh, editors. *Self-Injurious Behavior: Analysis, Assessment, and Treatment.* New York: Springer-Verlag, 1992.

Marziali, E., and H. Munroe-Blum. *Interpersonal Group Therapy for Borderline Personality Disorder.* New York: Basic Books, 1994.

Miller, D. *Women Who Hurt Themselves: A Book of Hope and Understanding.* New York: Basic Books, 1994.

Morgan, H. *Death Wishes? The Understanding and Management of Deliberate Self-Harm.* New York: Wiley, 1979.

Moskovitz, R. A. *Lost in the Mirror.* Dallas: Taylor Publishing, 1996.

Pipher, M. *Reviving Ophelia: Saving the Selves of Adolescent Girls.* New York: Ballentine Books, 1994.

Walsh, B. W., and P. M. Rosen. *Self-Mutilation: Theory, Research, and Treatment.* New York: Guilford Press, 1988.

APPENDIX

GLOSSARY

Borderline personality disorder: A disorder characterized by a pattern of unstable relationships, impulsiveness, recurrent suicidal behavior, and sudden or dramatic shifts in self-image. Many of the traits and statistics common to self-mutilation can also be seen in people with borderline personality disorder.

Dialectical behavioral therapy: Therapy that focuses on reducing self-injurious and life-threatening behaviors, DBT maintains that some people react abnormally to emotional stimulation, due to invalidating environments or unknown biological factors, and teaches people how to properly deal with stress.

Dissociative identity disorder: Dissociation is a mental process that disconnects a person's thoughts, memories, feelings, actions, or sense of identity from the present. Dissociative identity disorder can be brought on by a trauma and can cause people to become forgetful, while enduring periods of amnesia, blackouts, and a severe inability to function in daily activities.

Eating disorders: Common among those who self-injure, eating disorders include: anorexia nervosa (starving the body); bulimia (binge eating followed by purging, or throwing up); and compulsive overeating.

Interpersonal Group Therapy: A form of therapy that involves a group, rather than a one-on-one approach, in which each member describes a social situation faced in the past week and how he or she dealt with it. Guided by a therapist, the members of the group discuss each situation, come up with an acceptable response, and then share ways to deal with frustration or problems.

Major self-mutilation: The most extreme and rarest form of self-injury, major self-mutilation involves the damage or removal of large amounts of tissue, such as amputation or castration, and often results in permanent disfigurement. Perpetrators of this form of self-injury are often in a psychotic state or are extremely intoxicated.

Neurotransmitters: Chemicals that pass messages to and from nerve cells. Neurotransmitters are a key component in the passing of information from the body (pain, pleasure, warmth, etc.) to the brain and throughout the central nervous system.

Obsessive-compulsive disorder: A disorder commonly linked with self-injury, obsessive-compulsive disorder is characterized by recurrent obsessions (recurring and persistent ideas, thoughts, impulses, or images) or compulsions that are severe and cause the person distress or impairment. Obsessive-compulsive disorder is believed to be caused by a serotonin imbalance in the brain.

Post-traumatic stress disorder: Another disorder commonly associated with self-mutilation, this disorder occurs after an extreme event—such as sexual or child abuse, war, physical attack or torture, diagnosis of a life-threatening disease, or natural disasters. Symptoms of post-traumatic stress disorder include: distressing and intrusive memories and dreams, withdrawal from people or places that remind the person of the traumatic event, or intense anxiety, anger, and irritability.

Psychosocial: Relating social conditions to mental health.

Psychotherapy: A type of treatment for mental disorders and behavioral disturbances. Clinicians attempt to modify a person's behavior through techniques such as support, suggestion, reeducation, and reassurance, rather than through use of drugs.

Rational emotive therapy: Based upon the principal that feelings control thoughts, this form of therapy teaches a person that he or she can learn to control his or her anger and negative emotions by learning to rethink situations.

Self-injury: The deliberate damaging of one's body without the intent to commit suicide. Types of self-injury include cutting, burning, or beating. Known by other names, including self-mutilation, self-injury has three classifications: major self-mutilation, stereotypic self-mutilation, and superficial self-mutilation.

Serotonin: A type of neurotransmitter found in the blood serum and mucus of mammals that causes the blood vessels to narrow. Serotonin has been linked to regulating emotion, mood, impulsivity, aggression, digestion, smooth muscle relaxation, and sexual behavior. Decreases in the body's serotonin level have been linked to increased irritation and aggression.

Stereotypic self-mutilation: Fixed, often rhythmic and repetitive, patterns of self-injury, such as head banging or biting oneself. Stereotypic self-mutilation is most commonly seen in the institutionalized mentally retarded, but it also occurs in autistic, psychotic, or schizophrenic people.

Superficial self-mutilation: The most common form of self-mutilation, this type occurs occasionally, rather than regularly, mostly among emotionally-distressed teenage girls. While the injuries sustained through cutting, carving, or burning the flesh usually do not result in major tissue damage, superficial self-mutilation can become addictive, resulting in scarring, and can become an overwhelming preoccupation for its victim.

Synapses: Connection point in the central nervous system at which nervous impulses pass from one nerve cell to another. The word comes from the Greek word *synapsis*, which means "junction."

Trichotillomania: Compulsive pulling of head and body hair. This trait is linked to obsessive-compulsive disorder.

APPENDIX

INDEX

APPENDIX

PICTURE CREDITS

page

8: PhotoDisc Vol. 59 #59026

10: Telegraph Colour Library/FPG International

13: AP/Wide World Photos

14: AP/Wide World Photos

16: Kathy Sloane/Photo Researchers, Inc.

19: AP/Wide World Photos

20: PhotoDisc Vol. 59 #59238

22: Susan Rosenberg/Photo Researchers, Inc.

24: AP/Wide World Photos

26: PhotoDisc Vol. 25 #25302

28: Jim Cummins/FPG International

32: PhotoDisc Vol. 45 #45017

33: Shirley Zeiberg/Photo Researchers, Inc.

34: David M. Grossman/Photo Researchers, Inc.

37: PhotoDisc Vol. 25 #25299

39: Ron Chapple/FPG International

42: Susan Rosenberg/Photo Researchers, Inc.

44: Cleo Photography/Photo Researchers, Inc.

47: Richard T. Nowitz/Photo Researchers, Inc.

48: © Shirley Zeiberg Photography

50: © Shirley Zeiberg Photography

53: Telegraph Colour Library/FPG International

54: PhotoDisc Vol. 59 #59156

56: © Carolyn McKeone/Photo Researchers, Inc.

58: © Shirley Zeiberg Photography

60: PhotoDisc Vol. 45 #45091

62: PhotoDisc Vol. 45 #45086

64: PhotoDisc Vol. 24 #24224

67: © Joseph Szabo/Photo Researchers, Inc.

70: Richard T. Nowitz/Photo Researchers, Inc.

72: Renee Lynn/Photo Researchers, Inc.

75: Erika Stone/Photo Researchers, Inc.

Senior Consulting Editor Carol C. Nadelson, M.D., is president and chief executive officer of the American Psychiatric Press, Inc., staff physician at Cambridge Hospital, and Clinical Professor of Psychiatry at Harvard Medical School. In addition to her work with the American Psychiatric Association, which she served as vice president in 1981–83 and president in 1985–86, Dr. Nadelson has been actively involved in other major psychiatric organizations, including the Group for the Advancement of Psychiatry, the American College of Psychiatrists, the Association for Academic Psychiatry, the American Association of Directors of Psychiatric Residency Training Programs, the American Psychosomatic Society, and the American College of Mental Health Administrators. In addition, she has been a consultant to the Psychiatric Education Branch of the National Institute of Mental Health and has served on the editorial boards of several journals. Doctor Nadelson has received many awards, including the Gold Medal Award for significant and ongoing contributions in the field of psychiatry, the Elizabeth Blackwell Award for contributions to the causes of women in medicine, and the Distinguished Service Award from the American College of Psychiatrists for outstanding achievements and leadership in the field of psychiatry.

Consulting Editor Claire E. Reinburg, M.A., is editorial director of the American Psychiatric Press, Inc., which publishes about 60 new books and six journals a year. She is a graduate of Georgetown University in Washington, D.C., where she earned bachelor of arts and master of arts degrees in English. She is a member of the Council of Biology Editors, the Women's National Book Association, the Society for Scholarly Publishing, and Washington Book Publishers.

Ann Holmes has written and edited professionally for over 15 years. Her special areas of interest are both cultural and medical topics. Her books include *The Mental Effects of Heroin* and *Psychological Effects of Cocaine and Crack Addiction* in Chelsea House Publishers' ENCYCLOPEDIA OF PSYCHOLOGICAL DISORDERS. Ann and her family live in southwestern Pennsylvania, where she edits *The Loyalhanna Review*, the literary journal of the Ligonier Valley Writers.